I hope you enjoy
Be cool... stay in school :)

TEACHINGS BY
MILOU

MONTHS OF THE YEAR

Denise Duguay

MONTHS OF THE YEAR

It takes **12 months**
to make a year

Milou will teach
you so it's clear.

Once you're done,
show Mom & Dad

What you've learned,
they'll be so glad.

January

January is the **first** month of the year

The first day is fireworks and cheer.

They're very loud and very bright

And fully light up the starry night.

February

February is the **second** month of the year

The 14th is Valentine's Day for lovers so dear.

We express our love to family and friends

Because to us, they're precious gems.

MARCH

March is the **third** month of the year

Hurray, hurray, March Break is here.

We play, we run, we have fun in the snow

With sleds and skates, we go, go, go.

APRIL

April is the **fourth** month of the year

The Easter Bunny will soon be here.

Baskets, chocolates, and treats alike

But Milou hopes for a shiny new bike.

May

May is the **fifth** month of the year

Beautiful flowers start to appear.

It's also the month for Mother's Day

So say "I love you" in your own special way.

June

June is the **sixth** month of the year

The last month of a long school year.

Father's Day has arrived once again

So show him you love him like only you can.

July

July is the **seventh** month of the year

It's Canada's birthday, so let's all cheer.

Fly your flag with joy and pride

With family and friends at your side.

August

August is the **eighth** month of the year

We go to the beach with our swimming gear.

We play, we swim, and splash all around

So much fun, it's hard to calm down.

September

September is the **ninth** month of the year

Oh, no, school time is here.

Playtime is over, it's now time to learn

And answer class questions, turn by turn.

October

October is the **tenth** month of the year

Yippee, yippee, Halloween is here.

All dressed up with bag in hand

Trick or treat is the command.

November

November is the **eleventh** month of the year

A time to remember our soldiers so dear.

So wear your poppy with great pride

To show your thanks to those who died.

December

December is the **twelfth** month of the year

Rudolph and Santa are finally here.

Boys and girls near and far

Wish for toys on the northern star.

Milou
is done teaching you

All the months you
never knew.

Practice hard and
you'll remember

The months from
January to **December**.

Suite 300 - 990 Fort St
Victoria, BC, V8V 3K2
Canada

www.friesenpress.com

Copyright © 2018 by Denise Duguay
First Edition — 2018

All rights reserved.

No part of this publication may be reproduced in any form, or by any means, electronic or mechanical, including photocopying, recording, or any information browsing, storage, or retrieval system, without permission in writing from FriesenPress.

ISBN
978-1-5255-1608-5 (Hardcover)
978-1-5255-1609-2 (Paperback)
978-1-5255-1610-8 (eBook)

1. JUVENILE NONFICTION, REFERENCE

Distributed to the trade by The Ingram Book Company

CPSIA information can be obtained
at www.ICGtesting.com
Printed in the USA
LVHW01s0151260518
578581LV00002B/2/P